NEW
NATURAL
BEAUTY

For Paddy
Facile princeps

ACKNOWLEDGMENTS
I should like to thank all those who shared their valuable knowledge with me whilst researching and writing this book. In particular, I am grateful to Len and Shirley Price, Pat Suthers, Jan Kusmerick of Fragrant Earth and also to Geraldine Howard of Aromatherapy Associates for their aromatherapy expertise and valuable information on essential oils. I must also thank my saintly mother, who twice-tested every natural beauty recipe, Andrew Harrison MRPharmS for his technical advice, and my talented researchers Sarah Hamilton-Fleming and Karen Swan-MacLeod for their additional in-put. My gratitude also to Iain Philpott for his cover photography, hairdresser Terence Renati and make-up artist Vicki Partridge.

Note
This book is a reference guide. The suggestions given are not intended to be a substitute for medical advice or treatment. Any application of the ideas or recommendations in this book is at the reader's own discretion.

Liz Earle

NEW
NATURAL
BEAUTY

LIMITED EDITIONS
BOOKTITLES

INTRODUCTION

We all use some sort of skincare — be it a swift scrub with soap and water or some of the more sophisticated age-defying day creams. Modern cosmetology is shrouded in technical mystery and yet the formulae for many of our health and beauty remedies today are based on traditional techniques that have been handed down over the generations. In fact, modern scientific research is now endorsing much of the folklore surrounding natural therapies that have been used for centuries.

Making your own health and beauty preparations is fun and easy to follow. It can also save a great deal of money. Water and alcohol are the two most commonly used skincare ingredients, so why pay pounds for a product that contains only a few pence worth of ingredients? Unless you choose products that contain genuinely high levels of natural ingredients, you may be better off with homemade remedies. These can contain much more useful amounts of active ingredients such as essential fatty acids, vitamins and enzymes. In addition, you may tailor many lotions and potions to suit your own individual needs and make many remedies for yourself, your family and friends.

The recipes in this book range from simple blends of massage oils to more detailed descriptions of making soap and skin cream, for the more adventurous. Effective treatments for skin problems such as acne, eczema, psoriasis and ageing skin are also included. You will find practical background information on all the ingredients used and where you can obtain them. Unlike many shop-bought toiletries, your own products avoid animal testing and you can choose to buy cruelty-free ingredients. You can also re-cycle containers and cut down on the enormous amount of packaging waste produced by commercial manufacturers.

With the help of this book you will be able to transform your kitchen into a beauty playground and fill your bathroom shelves with therapeutic treatments for your face, hair and entire body.

Liz Earle

NATURAL BEAUTY
IN HISTORY

Natural beauty care has played an important part in history, since the earliest civilisations when mankind first used many of the plants and other elements provided by nature. The pioneers of natural beauty treatments were probably the cave people living in the Mesolithic period around 10,000 BC, who applied grease and castor oil to soften the skin, and tattooed their bodies with plant dyes as protection from the sun. Recorded formulae for skin softening lotions date back to Biblical times, where women made lotions from olive oil and spices which were often rubbed into sore feet to keep them smooth and supple. Scented barks and dried roots were finely ground to make talcum powders and precious aromatic oils were often rubbed into the hair to keep it smelling sweet.

EGYPTIAN LIPS

The first lipsticks were made in the ancient city of Ur, near Babylon, some 5000 years ago. Next door in Egypt, Cleopatra relied on several hundreds of natural beauty remedies to maintain her legendary powers of seduction. Her fragrances may have literally changed the face of history as Mark Antony was intoxicated by the scent of rose and patchouli oils on her skin. Cleopatra's beauty routine included bathing in ass's milk and applying face packs made from crushed sesame seeds and barley. Like most Egyptian women, she also favoured the use of henna and walnut oil to keep her hair dark and glossy, and used black kohl crayons made from powdered antimony (a type of metal) around her eyes to dramatic effect. Her shimmering blue and green eyeshadows were made from finely ground semi-precious stones such as lapis lazuli and malachite, which had a practical as well as cosmetic purpose as they shielded the skin from the sun's strong rays. Less appealing were Cleopatra's

lipsticks and rouge which came from the deep red pigment of finely crushed carmine beetles and powdered ant's eggs.

The women of Thebes and those who lived alongside the Nile were reputed to be the most beautiful in the world and they certainly made full use of the many natural paints and powders for their face, body and hair. Egyptian queens and noblewomen were buried with scores of alabaster jars filled with lotions and potions to use on every part of the body. A cosmetic chest was also included for the after-life and contained sticks of kohl to outline their eyes, beeswax mascara and mirrors made from highly polished copper set into carved ivory handles.

Compared to other cultures of that time, the Egyptians were extremely vain and prided themselves on their appearance. It is no coincidence that cosmetics were first developed by the Ancient Egyptians and drawings depicting the extensive use of elaborate eye make-up have been found in tombs built as far back as 5000 BC. Surprisingly, remains of eye make-up found in the pyramids show that it was often made from fairly harsh substances, such as lead sulphide and charcoal which would have irritated their eyes. Reddish brown face paints contained clays with a high iron content to give them their colour, and there was even an anti-wrinkle remedy made from bullock's bile and ostrich eggs! Fortunately, these natural remedies have not stood the test of time, although many other Egyptian innovations remain relevant.

ORIGINAL SKIN

The Ancient Egyptians can probably take the credit for devising most of the earliest beauty preparations and they were especially fond of highly aromatic perfumes. Relics found in the pyramids include precious perfume flasks and essential oil carriers, placed there to keep their owners smelling sweet in the after-life. Aromatic oils were sold by Arab traders who travelled across the Middle East with precious cargoes of spices, frankincense and myrrh strapped to their camels. These were highly prized and were worth even more than gold. We can learn a great deal of useful information from the beauty recipes that have been handed down from years gone by.

In addition to cosmetics and perfumes, the Ancient Egyptians were the first to develop soap, made from a natural cleanser called saponin, which is extracted from the soaproot or soapwort plant. They also added animal fats and fragrant oils to the soap formula and used them for household cleaning as well as bathing. The Assyrians in the Middle East added precious perfumed oils too, to their washing water and were scrupulous about personal hygiene. Body-smoothing products were popular and skin scrubs first made their appearance around 1000 BC. These were made from powdered pumice stone and used by Assyrian women to buff the body and keep the skin smooth. Before showering (which they did frequently), the Egyptians and Assyrians would rub themselves with handfuls of sand to clean the pores.

BRAIDS AND BEARDS

Both the Assyrian men and women took great pride in their hair and it was always worn elaborately braided, oiled and perfumed. Tiny balls of perfumed wax were tucked close to the scalp so that during long banquets the fragrance would be released by body heat and trickle down the neck to last throughout the evening. Men kept their beards trimmed like topiary into exotic shapes, and facial hair was such an important symbol of strength and power that several Egyptian queens took to wearing a false gilded beard on ceremonial occasions.

Applying make-up for a night out obviously took a great deal of time, as is illustrated by the cosmetic box of Thuthu, the wife of a nobleman, kept in the British Museum. It contains the following necessities: sandals, elbow pads (for resting on, as putting on make-up was a lengthy process), pumice stones to smooth the skin and remove body hair, eye pencils of wood and ivory to apply powdered colour, a bronze dish for mixing colours and three pots of face cream.

The Ancient Greeks also knew a thing or two about cosmetics, although their mascara made from a mixture of gum and soot does seem a bit crude. Greek women painted their cheeks with herbal pastes made from crushed berries and seeds to give them a healthy looking glow. They also developed a more dangerous habit of using white lead and mercury on their faces, to give the complexion a chalky appearance. Unbeknown to them, these heavy metals were absorbed through the skin and resulted in many untimely deaths — an unfortunate trend which continued down the ages.

The Greek physician Galen recognised the problem and wrote, 'women who often paint themselves with mercury, though they be very young, they presently turn old and withered and have wrinkled faces like an ape'. As well as being a first-class physician, Galen is also credited with the original recipe for cold cream, based on beeswax, olive oil and rose-water. He also remarked that garden snails, when finely ground, made an effective mois-turiser and the unfortunate creatures were used in beauty preparations for several cen-turies. Less unpleasant Greek customs included using natural henna to stain finger and toe-nails red in much the same way as we paint ours with polish today. They also made false eyebrows from dyed goat's hair, which they attached to the skin with nat-ural gums and resins.

It was the Romans, however, who established many of our modern beauty habits. As the Roman Empire swept through Europe it left behind a legacy of daily bathing in communal baths scented with rosewater.

The Romans also intro-duced the habit of regular shaving for men, with razors made from sharpened bronze. Rich noble-men and women continued to bathe in ass's milk and Nero's Queen Poppeia travelled with her own string of donkeys to provide the milk for her baths. Roman noblewomen also popularised the use of natural cosmetics in Britain by wearing kohl around their eyes, painting their cheeks with red paste made from beetle shells and rubbing sweet-smelling aromatic oils into their hair.

One aspect of their appearance which took up a great deal of time, was the dyeing and dressing of their hair. The Romans used many different types of natural hair dyes, including one made from the mineral quick-lime, which gave their hair a lustrous, red-dish-gold tinge. Walnut oil made by steeping walnut shells in olive oil was also used to keep the hair dark brown when it began to turn grey. In Ancient Rome, blonde hair was initially considered to be a symbol of a pros-titute, but with the arrival of the Scandinavian slave girls, noblewomen began to dye their own naturally dark hair lighter shades of blonde using a concentrated infusion of saf-fron flowers. Rosemary and juniper were the main ingredients in hair tonics reputed to prevent hair loss, and emollient skin soothers were made from saffron flowers and beeswax.

Pliny the Elder also records the use of many natural beauty ingredients, including quince cream from Cos, saffron from Rhodes and rosewater from Phaselis. He also notes the extensive use of *chypre* from Cyprus, a musky, long-lasting perfume. Many of these ingredients are still present in modern cosmetics and can be used in several effective homemade remedies. Other natural ingredi-ents that have fortunately not stood the test of time quite so well include crocodile dung which, believe it or not, was a popular Roman face pack.

BEAUTY IN BRITAIN

When the Romans invaded Britain they were appalled to find that the native inhabitants did not believe in bathing and quickly set about building communal baths, some of which still exist in spa towns such as Bath (hence its name). However, once they had departed Britain during the fourth century, the practice of regular bathing died out, except for the occasional cold water plunge undertaken as a penance. Despite this lack of routine cleanliness, women during the Middle Ages did continue to wear some form of make-up, although rouge was only worn by shady ladies of the night.

Noblewomen continued to use white lead on their faces; they plucked their eyebrows and stained their lips dark red with plant dyes.

Natural skincare remedies were also popular and most noblewomen had their own favourite recipes for keeping the complexion smooth. To combat the destructive effects of wearing lead paste on the face, masks were made using ground asparagus roots and goat's milk, which were rubbed into the skin with pieces of warm bread. Elaborate braided hair styles were also popular and a kind of hair gel was made from a mixture of swallow droppings and lizard tallow.

During the Crusades, knights returned home with all kinds of exotic preparations never before seen in Britain. Essential oils became popular as perfumes and were also used as antiseptics to ward off the plague. The technique of soap-making was also imported from Italy, although for centuries to come soap was mainly used for washing dishes and clothes, not bodies.

THE RENAISSANCE

The next era to literally change the face of history was the Renaissance, a period of great learning and cultural development which saw many improvements in the world of natural beauty. Ladies in Venice, including Catherine de Medici, even established their own society for cosmetic testing and beauty training. However, their new-found knowledge did not stop them from continuing to use the destructive lead paint on their faces, neck and cleavage. One new invention was the beauty spot, originally made from small circles of black velvet, used to hide blemishes, such as warts, pimples and pox scars.

The philosophy of personal hygiene was also gaining ground and the first commercial toothpowders appeared, usually made from a mixture of dried sage, nettles and powdered clay. In the 1500s, Venetian noblewomen would also dye their hair by applying lotions derived from saffron flowers or sulphur and baking them on to their heads by sitting in the hot summer sun.

Although the Europeans in general were still suspicious of regular bathing (they believed that it weakened the body) they used a great deal of perfume, presumably to mask the inevitably unpleasant smell of body odour. In 1508 one of the first European perfumeries was set up by monks of the Dominican Brotherhood in Florence. They produced many popular fragrances included rhubarb elixir and melissa water, and developed scented orris powder made from ground iris roots, which were used to perfume clothes and household linen.

A FRAGRANT REIGN

Queen Elizabeth I imported many Italian and French fragrances, including scented kid gloves which were made in the hillside village of Grasse in the south of France. Life in Grasse originally revolved around the tannery industry, but perfume quickly became more popular then gloves and other leather goods, so the village turned into one of the leading fragrance centres in the world. Queen Elizabeth I was also one of Britain's most celebrated users of natural beauty preparations and her many portraits illustrate her passion for red wigs and painted skin.

Meanwhile, Elizabethan ladies still used white lead face paint and toxic mercury sulphide for rouge. Horace Walpole later wrote of 'that pretty young woman, Lady Fortrose . . . at point of death, killed like Lady Coventry and others of white lead, of which nothing could break her.' Lady Coventry herself was only twenty-seven when she died from lead poisoning absorbed through her skin. The poisonous white lead was mixed with vinegar to form a paste called ceruse. The finest was thought to come from Venice and was very expensive. The less wealthy fared much better as they had to use cheaper, safer alternatives made from sulphur and borax. White lead made the hair fall out and the extensive use of ceruse throughout the Elizabethan era explains the fashion for high foreheads, as hairlines were eroded.

Another reason for hair loss was the use of the corrosive oil of vitriol (sulphuric acid) mixed with rhubarb juice as a hair tonic and lightener. Lipsticks were a somewhat safer blend of cochineal and beeswax, and finely ground mother-of-pearl became popular as an iridescent eyeshadow. Although bathing was not fashionable, the ladies of the court did take care to keep their complexions clean. The great Queen herself washed her face alternately in red wine and ass's milk, while others used rainwater or even their urine.

Herbal infusions were also used to keep the skin clear, including fennel and eyebright water. On the rare occasions when their hair was cleaned, it was not washed but dry shampooed using finely powdered clays that were combed through to absorb the build-up of grease and dirt. Whisked egg whites were used to tighten and glaze the skin, and beauty spots remained a popular ploy for concealing blemishes. Freckles were frowned upon and one remedy for their removal calls for an infusion of elder leaves mixed with birch sap and brimstone (sulphur) to be applied to the skin by moonlight and removed in the morning with fresh butter. Bear's grease was a popular base for rouge and skin creams, and make-up pencils were made by mixing plaster of Paris with plant pigments to form sticks, which were dried in the sun.

During the reign of Charles I, the first British toiletry company set up shop in London. A young Mr Yardley is recorded as paying the monarch a large sum to gain the concession to manufacture soap for the whole of the capital. Unfortunately, the records of his activities were destroyed in the Great Fire of London, in 1666, but we do know that Yardley used lavender as the main perfume ingredient. From this time on, skin-care remedies became increasingly refined and ladies of the court of James II used moisturisers made from spices and vanilla pods infused in honey. However, the use of lead-based ceruse on the complexions continued, so the trend for high foreheads and an absence of eyebrows was still fashionable. Children had their brows covered in walnut oil to decrease hair growth and eyebrows were shaved and replaced with more delicate versions made from mouse skin. Balls of fine shaving soap also appeared for the men, who would have visited a cut-throat barber for their daily shave.

In 1786 an Act of Parliament was passed to tax cosmetics, and from this we can derive an accurate list of what was available at the time. The cosmetics listed include essences, powders, wash balls and pomades such as 'tincture of peach kernels', 'essence of bouquet' and 'carnation of lilies'. Make-up pigments included rouge, blanche, vegetable rouge (made from the safflower thistle) and serviette rouge (applied to the cheeks with a small cloth). There was also 'liquid bloom of roses', 'cold cream' and 'beautifying cream'.

THE WIG REVOLUTION
By the time of the French Revolution in 1789, natural cosmetics for both men and women of the Court were the height of fashion. Elaborate powdered wigs, rouge and face powder were used extensively, with the men often wearing far more than the women.

Although shampoo had by now been invented, it was common for courtiers to keep their natural hair short and unwashed while wearing a wig on top. These were often so large that several unfortunate noblewomen died from burns suffered when their headpieces brushed passed the candlelit chandeliers. As the wigs were made from a mass of wool and animal grease they were highly combustible and a huge fire risk. The wigs were extremely expensive and children were employed to sit on an adult's shoulders and snatch them from the heads of courtiers as they rode past in their open carriages.

From this time onwards it became fashionable to appear pale and interesting, and women's fashions focused on flimsy muslin dresses which were both diaphanous and daring. Sometimes they were even dampened to make them cling, often resulting in bronchitis and pneumonia for the unfortunate wearer. However, as the Empress Josephine had an olive complexion (she was brought up in the West Indies), she continued to make herbal rouge an essential fashion accessory.

One of the first beauty boutiques to supply the Parisian courtiers was opened in 1828 by Pierre Guerlain, founder of the famous French fragrance house. His shop was on the ground floor of the Hotel Maurice, in the Rue de Rivoli, where the dining room stands today. The many fragrant blends he created for the French Court included such patriotic perfumes as Bouquet Napoleon, Parfum de France and Eau Imperial (which is still available today). French noblewomen have a tradition of setting beauty trends and Empress Eugenie, the beautiful wife of Napoleon III, was among the first to wear and popularise mascara made from waxes and natural plant pigments.

HERBS AND HERBALISM
Over the centuries, herbalism and the study of plants had developed into an important

medical science. One of the first to document the medicinal and beautifying properties of herbs was Master-Surgeon John Gerard, who was an enthusiastic botanist as well as a respected physician.

One of his great medical advances was to identify the herb called scurvy-grass *Cochlearia officinalis*, which is rich in vitamin C and an effective cure for scurvy.

According to Gerard, the plant grew alongside the banks of the river Thames and along stretches of southern coastline – the very places where it was needed by the thousands of sailors who died from vitamin C deficiency.

In 1590, Gerard wrote a guide to herbalism which became a household bible throughout the country. Just like a well-thumbed cookery book today, Gerard's work was referred to almost daily for homemade herbal health and beauty recipes.

Probably the best-known English herbalist was Nicholas Culpeper. Born in 1616 the son of a Surrey rector, Culpeper studied Latin and medicine at Cambridge and might have gone on to become a doctor had his personal life not gone awry. After falling in love with a local girl, he borrowed £200 from his mother and ran away to get married. Culpeper arranged to meet his fiancée in Lewes, Sussex, but on the way there she was struck by lightning in a freak accident and killed. The distraught Culpeper abandoned his studies until eventually his grandfather set him up as an apprentice in a busy

London apothecary's practice. After his training, he turned his back on the lucrative medical world and opened a small shop in the deprived area of Spitalfields. Instead of prescribing expensive medicines he made 'cheap but wholesome medicines . . . not sending them to the East Indies for drugs, when they may fetch better out of their own gardens'.

Culpeper believed that common herbs could be used to great effect in medicine and revived many of the teachings of the Ancient Greek physicians such as Hippocrates and Galen. One of his favourite Biblical quotes was from Ecclesiastes: 'The Lord hath created Medicines out of the earth; and he that is wise will not abhor them'.

In 1649, Culpeper translated the *London Pharmacopoeia* into English from its original Latin – a move that outraged many doctors who preferred to keep their art secret. He went on to write his hugely popular book, *Culpeper's Complete Herbal*, which was first published in the 1600s and has been reprinted throughout the centuries until the latest edition in 1979. The book included many skincare remedies, such as an infusion of vervain and broom stalks to cleanse the skin, oatmeal boiled with vinegar to treat spots and pimples, and wheat bread soaked in rosewater to soothe tired eyes. He also recommended woodbine ointment for sunburn, thistle juice for hair loss and rosemary oil for spots.

One of the most popular books was *The Art of Beauty*, written in 1825 by an anonymous author who was quite likely to have been a doctor. Advice for ladies included erasing wrinkles by becoming overweight, applying powdered mint to reduce a large bosom and using belladonna juice from the deadly nightshade plant to enlarge the pupils of the eyes. The author also advises us not to put stays on children and to avoid tight corsets when pregnant.

A RIGID REGIME

But the doctrine for 'beauty training' makes modern health farms look like a holiday camp. Regency ladies were advised to observe the following regime:

- **Rise at six a.m.** (or five a.m. but not sooner). Briskly walk two to three miles examining the flora, fauna and clouds as you go. On returning home, change if you have perspired and dry your feet. Have all your skin, particularly that of the stomach, well rubbed with a cloth or flesh brush. Wash hands and face in cold water.
- **Breakfast** Plain biscuit (not bread), broiled underdone beefsteak or mutton chop with no fat, and half a pint mild ale.
- **Morning occupation** Out of doors, walk, garden, romp etc.
- **Dinner at two p.m.** As breakfast (no vegetables, boiled meat, fruit, sweets or pastry) plus the occasional mealy potato or boiled rice.
- **Afternoon occupation** Out of doors, walk, garden, romp etc.
- **Supper at seven p.m.** Much as breakfast and dinner.
- **Evening** At least an hour's active exercise.
- **Bedtime** Ten p.m. or earlier. Bathe feet in tepid water and rub as before.

The only advantages of this Spartan routine were to put colour back into the cheeks and to acknowledge the need to wash.

BRIGHTON BATHING

A fellow advocate of regular bathing at this time was the Prince Regent, later George IV, who installed an extensive bathroom at his Brighton Pavilion. Exclusively for men, the large tub was filled with a mixture of hot water and milk with herbs such as flax seeds (linseeds) to soften the skin. With the arrival of Queen Victoria on the throne came a new fervour for bathing throughout the country. However, there were no skin creams or cosmetics in polite society and only a dab of eau de cologne was deemed respectable. When out of doors, complexions were always protected by green veils (white netting reflected the sun and encouraged its rays) and by wearing bonnets with big brims. Inside, the face was shielded from the glare of the fire by decorated pole screens.

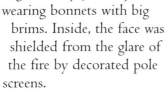

A CLEAN SWEEP

While the Victorians thoroughly disapproved of vanity they viewed cleanliness as being next to godliness. Soap became more widely available for those who could afford to buy it, although it was not until the middle of the century that most houses were built with indoor bathrooms. Until then, baths were taken in a tin tub in front of the sitting-room fire. At this time, soap was readily available but was sold in long anonymous bars sliced on the grocer's counter.

The first commercial soap was produced in 1884 by a Lancashire grocer called William Hesketh Lever. He had the brainwave of pre-cutting manufactured bars of soap, and stamping them with the brand name Sunlight. Demand soon overtook production and in 1888 William Lever bought a stretch of Mersey marshland and put Port Sunlight on the map of Britain. Although it sounds obvious today, William Lever's idea to give a bar of household soap a memorable name, package it properly and sell it energetically

was an entirely new marketing concept.

From these humble beginnings rose many other well-known soap brands, such as Lux, Lifebuoy and Shield – and so the mighty multinational detergent giant Lever Brothers was born. Even today, this company remains the largest supplier of soaps in the world.

Queen Victoria herself may have disapproved, but many other toiletry companies were founded during the Victorian era, including Coty and Cyclax. Yardley continued to go from strength to strength and had branched out from cakes of lavender soap into a skincare range that included Milady Powders, Lavender Vanishing Cream and Lavender Cold Cream.

Ideas for marketing and advertising began to emerge and Yardley adopted as its trademark an illustration of a group of flower sellers, with the girls holding primroses and not bunches of lavender.

At the end of the Victorian era a more relaxed attitude was taken to make-up and publications such as *Vogue* and *Queen* (now *Harpers & Queen*) magazine started to support the infant cosmetic industry. Sarah Bernhardt was reported to add half a pound of marshmallow flowers and four pounds of bran to her baths each day. She also endorsed Bernhardt Wrinkle Eradicator, a cream made from aluminium, almond milk and rosewater.

Across the Channel, Helena Rubinstein had left her native Poland and opened a salon in Paris where she sold a moisturiser called Crème Valaze. Helena was the eldest of eight sisters renowned for their beautiful complexions, and her skin cream – made by a pair of Polish chemists – became the cornerstone of what would later become her cosmetic empire.

Another Parisian contemporary of Helena Rubinstein was François Coty, a perfumier who was struggling to get his fragrances accepted in Paris. His big break came, quite literally, in 1903 when he unsuccessfully tried to get one of the larger shops to stock his scent. The manager refused even to open the bottle, but on the way out Coty smashed the bottle on the floor, the customers liked what they smelt and he was in business.

America was also busy building its own cosmetic empires and one of the first was established by Charles Meyer in 1860. A German wigmaker, Mr Meyer set up a small shop on Broadway selling Leichner's theatrical make-up, the first grease paint make in the USA. But a grease-based make-up requires something to remove it with, and for this, Pond's Extract was used — first distributed in 1846 by Theron T. Pond and later to become famous as Pond's Cold Cream.

At the turn of the century it was also discovered that zinc oxide made a good face powder which did not discolour or harm the skin, and in Hollywood, yet another immigrant wigmaker called Max Factor was making a name for himself designing make-up for the stars of the silent screen. Early movie-making was extremely primitive and stars of the black and white movies, such as Clara Bow, had to paint their faces with blue and brown panstick before their features could be clearly seen on the screen. Max Factor's Panchromatic make-up became so important to the stars of that age that it even won him an Academy Award in 1928.

As movie-making progressed, Max Factor discovered a demand for coloured pansticks and foundations for the colour 'talkies' and went on to invent a flesh-tinted make-up stick called 'Erase', which sold over 10 million units in its first year. His competitors included Elizabeth Arden, who had developed a range of make-up and skincare products based on natural ingredients. Elizabeth Arden herself was born in Canada and christened Florence Nightingale Graham — her name initially leading her to train as a nurse. However, she was so impressed by the well-groomed American women she came across that she retrained in a beauty salon. When she opened her own salon in New York's Fifth Avenue she searched for a more suitable name and was inspired by the book she was reading at the time called *Elizabeth and Her German Garden* by Elizabeth von Arnim, which contained verses from Tennyson's poem *Enoch Arden.*

Dorothy Gray was another American who opened a rival salon on Fifth Avenue, where she specialised in treatments for sensitive skins. Her massage treatments — which she carried out — were so popular that she insured her hands for a record US$100,000. Although Dorothy Gray's original skincare line has now disappeared, her name still appears on a range of toiletries made closer to home in Eastbourne, Sussex.

A longer-lived success story is that of Estée Lauder, one of the few women to become a legend in her own lifetime. Estée Lauder started up her business in 1946 by selling just four skincare products to the smart Saks Fifth Avenue department store in New York. From this humble beginning she founded the now world famous cosmetic company which she and her son Leonard still tightly control.

WARTIME REMEDIES

Back in Britain, however, the rigours of wartime rationing meant that there was very little in the way of glamorous make-up or beauty preparations. Women once again resorted to home remedies, including using gravy browning or strong tea to dye the legs in the absence of silk stockings. The restrictions on alcohol meant more concentrated perfumes and fewer eau de colognes were available and the lack of fats, oils and glycerine resulted in a shortage of skin creams.

Packaging was a problem for many manufacturers, with all the scrap metal being turned into munitions instead of make-up compacts. However, the beauty editor of *Queen* magazine did find time to mention Max Factor's Pan Cake make-up, recommending it 'particularly for women in the Forces or on other National work as it is very quick and easy to use and will stay on the skin for many hours . . . in six lovely shades from a pale flesh tint to a deep warm tan, in keeping with the colouring of the Woman's Service Uniforms.' A more important war-time purchaser of Pan Cake was the Ministry of Defence, who ordered specially formulated shades to darken the faces of commandos for night excursions.

After the war, developments in new cosmetics continued apace and throughout the fifties and sixties, make-up and skincare moved further away from Mother Nature and increasingly into the realms of technology. The concept of anti-ageing creams that might actually turn back the clock was introduced, together with its often ridiculously outlandish claims. Yet despite the catchy slogans and youthful models with artfully airbrushed skins, we have yet to encounter a skin cream that can cope with crow's feet.

In the last decade, the cosmetic and toiletry business has spent literally billions of dollars in search of the elusive elixir of youth that will wipe away all wrinkles. A whole variety of new ingredients have appeared on the scene, such as bovine collagen (made from cow fat), which claimed to be able to plump up the skin and give it a youthful appearance. The only problem with this is that the collagen molecules are far too large to penetrate even the uppermost layers of skin cells.

In a further refinement of technology, new 'delivery systems' were invented to carry complex ingredients into the skin where they might target ageing skin cells. Microscopically small liposomes were developed to slip through the surface of the skin where, in theory, they could release their cargo of active ingredients to individual skin cells. These active ingredients include a number of nutrients such as antioxidant vitamins, essential fatty acids, fruit acids and natural sugars.

Ironically, it has been the search for the most up-to-date and effective ingredients that has taken many cosmetic scientists back to nature's doorstep. Natural ingredients such as plant oils and herbal extracts, notably echinacea, are once again becoming increasingly popular as scientists begin to prove their legendary powers in the laboratory. Plant extracts such as chamomile have been found to heal damaged skin, avocado oil has been shown to regenerate ageing cells in mice and vitamins C and E are now known to be amongst the best anti-ageing ingredients of all times.

This is good news for us, as consumers. In fact, there has never been a better moment to combine the knowledge gathered by physicians, herbalists and beauticians over the last few thousand years and combine it with modern techniques to make the best natural beauty preparations for ourselves.

GETTING STARTED

The recipes for making your own natural beauty products are remarkably simple. You do not need to be a cosmetic scientist or have a degree in biotechnology to produce naturally effective products in your own kitchen. All the recipes have been tried and tested, but you may find some of the textures unusual. For example, the moisturising skin creams tend to be more concentrated than commercial lotions, as they have not been whipped with water and air to make them light. You may also find that some of the recipes vary according to the temperature, as ingredients such as coconut oil and cocoa butter are naturally harder in colder weather or if stored in a cool place.

This chapter lists the basic ingredients you will come across in the book, together with a description of how each one can be used. This means that you look up the properties of a particular ingredient and adapt a recipe to suit your own skin type, or devise your own concoctions in the future.

Many of the ingredients are probably sitting in your kitchen or bathroom right now. Others, such as herbs or fruits, can be grown in the garden or on a window sill to provide a year-round source of fresh ingredients. These are listed in more detail in The Botanicals chapter. If you have difficulty finding the more unusual ingredients, there is a list of stockists at the end of the book, as well as a glossary to explain the more technical terms.

USEFUL EQUIPMENT
Although there is little you need in the way of special equipment to start making your own beauty preparations, the following items will be helpful to have at hand. If you decide to make lots of your own recipes in the future, it might be worth keeping a set of utensils, such as spatulas, separate from the ones you use for cooking. This helps prevent the risk of cross-contamination of germs and odours, and means that your face cream will not end up smelling of onions!
- Plastic measuring spoons
- Set of small scales
- Heat-proof jugs or small bowls
- Enamel, stainless steel or Pyrex saucepan (not aluminium or cast iron, which can react with ingredients such as lemon juice)
- Fine mesh sieve
- Disposable coffee filters (to take tiny particles out of liquids)
- Small funnel for decanting liquids
- Rubber spatula or palette knife
- Metal mixing spoons (avoid wooden spoons, which absorb ingredients such as essential oils)
- Pipette (for measuring drop by drop, available from chemists)
Optional extras:
- Blender or food processor
- Pestle and mortar

The following are useful for packaging and storage:
- Selection of bottles and jars, preferably made from glass so they can be sterilised
- Sterilising fluid or tablets (from chemists)
- Spray bottles
- Paper towels (more hygienic than kitchen cloths for mopping up etc.)
- Sticky labels to name and date all items
- Cardboard boxes for storing finished items in the cool and dark (shoe boxes are ideal).

STORAGE TIPS
Unlike the needs of commercial beauty products, the recipes in this book do not contain added chemicals to prolong shelf-life. You will not find common skincare chemicals such as ethyl or isopropyl alcohols, parabens and ammonium compounds or benzoic acid

added to these natural remedies. However, steps must be taken to guard against bacterial or microbial spoilage and decomposition. Unfortunately, the basic oil and water mixture of many natural products is an excellent breeding ground for germs and a pot of cream is constantly exposed to new ones each time we dip our fingers into it.

Products most susceptible to spoilage include those made with fresh ingredients such as fruits and vegetables, although even these will usually keep for several days in the fridge. The quantities given for the recipes in this book are therefore designed to make relatively small amounts to avoid spoilage and subsequent wastage. Products stored in the fridge should be kept separate from food, such as in a salad drawer or in a cardboard box on the top shelf.

Make a habit of labelling every item with its name and the date of making so you know when to discard it. If in doubt — throw it out! Most skin creams can be safely stored in the bathroom cupboard, but keep them out of direct sunlight, which will encourage rancidity. A small disc of greaseproof paper placed on the top of each jar of cream helps to keep the air out and prolong shelf-life.

Adding vitamin E from capsules or from a few drops of wheatgerm oil also helps, as this nutrient acts as a natural preservative and prevents spoilage. Other natural preservatives include the antiseptic essential oils, notably lavender or menthol from peppermint, which have been added to beauty preparations for this reason for thousands of years.

HYGIENE HINTS

Bacteria love to breed in warm, moist conditions, so make life difficult for the bugs by keeping your equipment and preparation area as cool and dry as possible. All equipment, including final packing containers and lids,

must be sterilised by dipping in sterilising fluid before using (alternatively, use a mild bleach solution and rinse well in boiled water). Whenever a recipe calls for water, only use filtered, boiled then cooled water, or distilled water, which is available from the chemist. Some varieties of bottled water may also be used, but choose reputable brands that have stringent quality controls and use those with low levels of minerals such as sodium (salt). Plain tap water contains many unwanted extras such as nitrates, chlorine, fluoride, traces of pesticides etc. and should not be used at all. It sounds obvious, but always wash your hands before you start.

ALLERGY TESTING

Most natural skincare remedies are well-suited to those with sensitive skins as they do not contain the artificial colourants and fragrances that most often lead to allergic reactions. Perfume contains as many as two hundred separate chemical ingredients, any one of which can trigger an adverse skin reaction. However, natural does not always equal safe and it is important to remember that even some completely natural substances can be dangerous if they are not handled with knowledge and care. Substances such as arsenic and lead are totally natural, yet we would not dream of using them on the skin. Likewise, many herbs and plant extracts have powerful effects that should not be underestimated, and must be treated with respect.

In the lists that follow you will find more detailed information on the safety of some of the stronger ingredients. Also, bear in mind that your own skin may not suit a particular ingredient or recipe. Although less likely to cause an allergic reaction than many chemical fragrances or preservatives, even basic natural ingredients such as lanolin or lemon juice can pose a problem for a few people. For this reason, it is wise to carry out a patch test whenever trying an ingredient or recipe for the first time.

HOW TO DO A PATCH TEST

Apply a small amount of the substance to be tested on an area of fine skin, such as the inner elbow. Cover with a sticking plaster and leave in place overnight. Should any unusual reaction, such as itching or redness, occur, bathe the affected area with a weak bicarbonate of soda solution and apply a soothing ointment such as calendula cream. Keep a record of the recipes you have tested and the ingredients which you know are suited to your skin. This will save time re-testing new products made with ingredients that you know are safe for your skin type.

RAW MATERIALS

The following A to Z of ingredients can be found in chemists or health shops:

Acetone

A harsh, colourless liquid that should be used with great care. It is highly flammable and is used as a thinner for paints and varnishes, including nail polish. It can be used sparingly as an inexpensive nail polish remover, but a small amount of almond oil should be added before use as it is extremely drying. Used in large amounts, acetone can cause skin rashes, and inhaling its pungent fumes can also irritate your lungs. However, small quantities of neat acetone can be carefully dabbed on to spots and pimples with a cotton bud as its drying action will remove any excess sebum or oil.

Aloe Vera Juice

This succulent African plant looks like a spineless cactus and is reputed to have been used by Cleopatra as a skin cleanser. It is a member of the lily family and has fat, rubbery green leaves which produce a thick, clear, semi-solid gel when cut. Aloe vera juice is made from the plant's natural gel and has been analysed as being 99·5 per cent water. However, the remaining 0·5 per cent contains over twenty different amino acids and carbohydrates, and many magical properties are credited to the plant's unusual juice. It contains a number of therapeutically active compounds including glycosides (a sugar derivative), polysaccharides (complex carbohydrate molecules) and volatile oils.

Aloe vera juice soothes and softens the skin and can help heal severe burns. It is a common ingredient in first-aid skin creams, shampoos and natural bodycare products. Studies at the University of Pennsylvania Radiology Department have found that the juice of this plant is more effective in treating radiation burns than any other known product. As a result, the American army have stockpiled significant quantities to be used on troops in the event of a nuclear disaster.

Aloe vera juice is available in bottles from health shops and can be added to tonics and cleansers to soothe the skin. The best quality juice or gel available contains 96-100 per cent pure aloe. Look for those that have not been preserved with alcohol as this diminishes the aloe's unique healing properties.

Almond Oil

This colourless plant oil is extracted from the oil-enriched kernels of sweet, ripe almonds grown mainly in the Mediterranean. It is an important ingredient in moisturising soaps, creams and skin treatments and can even be used neat as a nourishing hand and nail massage oil. A refined form of almond oil is available from the chemist, and some supermarkets also sell a gourmet version of the oil that is suitable for skincare use.

Evenir
The ev
with v
evenin
the co
herb, :
tiny, c
of the
by fo:
it is c
been
The
whicl
A
are g
exter
tains
gam
rose
GL
Th
cut
mil
GL
dif
hel
tre
syr
tro

in
pr
cr
n
u
ti
a
y
t
e

Arnica Tincture

Made from the dried flowers of the arnica plant, arnica has many uses in skincare. It is an efficient skin soother and is especially useful for drawing out bruises or easing aches and sprains. Used for centuries by homoeopaths, arnica tincture is one of our most effective remedies for sore, swollen skin, but should not be applied to scratches or open wounds (see The Botanicals, page 39).

Avocado Oil

This traditional beauty oil was first used by the tribeswomen of Mexico and Arizona where the avocado pear tree grows wild. The avocado itself is a highly unusual fruit as it takes two years to ripen and its flesh contains nearly fifty per cent plant oil. The natural oil is highly nutritious and is a good source of vitamin E, magnesium, traces of the B complex vitamins and lecithin. Although high in calories, the avocado does not contain any cholesterol and is a good source of the fatty acid linoleic acid, which strengthens the membranes surrounding skin cells. Its stone also contains as yet unidentified substances that have been shown in some studies to help regenerate skin cells.

Generally, the darker the avocado oil the better, as this means that it has undergone minimum processing and is likely to retain more of its natural nutrients. Avocado oil has a nutty smell and is one of the best oils for soothing dry, parched skins. It is available in either liquid form or capsules, which can be pierced with a pin and added to skin creams.

Balm of Gilead

This tincture is extracted from the buds of the poplar tree, common in Asia and North America. These reddish brown buds are coated with a sticky resin that is collected and made into Balm of Gilead. Its use as a skin-soothing ingredient and also as a pleasantly pungent perfume has been documented since biblical times. Balm of Gilead contains a type of painkiller called salicin which is also found in aspirin and is used in medical herbalism as an antiseptic and stimulant, especially when treating coughs and colds. The tincture is also a mild circulatory stimulant and can be used in skin lotions to tone and strengthen the epidermis or upper layers of the skin, although it should not be used near the eyes or mouth.

Borax

This white powder consists of alkaline crystals and comes from a mineral that is mined in North and South America. It is a form of the trace mineral boron, which is used by the body to keep bones and teeth healthy and strong. Commonly used as a water softener, preservative and skin soother, borax also acts as an antiseptic, although it should not be

used c
prope
ucts i
moist
prope
some

Cala
This
the r
Acor
zinc
adde
The
and
also
som

Cas
Ext
gro
thi
pre
po
be
ca
br
ar
a sl
sl
fc
r

C
s

THE
BOTANICALS

In addition to the basic range of raw materials needed to make preparations to cleanse and protect our skin and hair, there is also a growing range of natural plant extracts that can be added to give products specific benefits. For example, a skin tonic may be created to suit a dry, sensitive skin by adding chamomile flowers, or a product may be made suitable for an oily, combination skin by including nettles and yarrow.

Herbal extracts are ideal for 'customising' a beauty recipe and adding a personal touch to skin creams or massage blends. You may also have a particular scent that you are fond of, such as rose or lavender, and these may be added to many of my recipes in the form of a few drops of fragrant essential oil.

PLANTS AND HERBS

The Romans were largely responsible for bringing many Mediterranean plants and herbs to Britain and for their subsequent wide-scale cultivation. They encouraged the use of plants and herbs in health and beauty preparations, as well as in perfumes and as salad or cooking ingredients. After the Roman Empire collapsed, herbs and herbal medicines fell out of favour, encouraged by the rise of Christianity which considered faith, penitence and prayer to be the only answers to illness. Herbs then became associated with witchcraft and many of the original herbalists had a difficult time in re-establishing their art.

However, many herbs and plants remain potent natural healers and have a wide range of uses in beauty preparations. For example, a variety of bullwort has been used for centuries for skin and kidney complaints, and it is now used in hospitals, together with ultraviolet light therapy, to treat severe skin conditions such as psoriasis and vitiligo. Even on a day-to-day level most modern skincare products still rely on herbal extracts that have been tried and tested over thousands of years.

The simplest way to ensure a steady supply of fresh herbs and plants, such as roses and geraniums, is to grow your own, either in the garden, in a window box or along a sunny window sill. Many extracts come from plants normally classed as weeds, such as stinging nettles, and these are remarkably easy to grow. In fact, without careful control, they will quickly take over the flowerbeds. Many flowers also have unusual properties that are especially useful in skincare. For example, marigolds give us a soothing calendula extract and geranium leaves contain one of the best natural perfumes.

When picking herbs and wild plants, avoid those that have been growing along a roadside or close to any source of industrial pollution. Plants are highly sensitive to pollutants in the atmosphere and quickly absorb them into their petals and leaves. If growing or gathering your own supplies sounds too much like hard work, dried herbs and flower heads are readily available from herbal suppliers (there is a list of these at the back of this book). Fresh herbs are also increasingly available from supermarkets and greengrocers, but do not be tempted to use flowers from the florist as these blooms are often sprayed with powerful herbicides which will harm the skin.

The most useful plants for cosmetic and beauty preparations are alphabetically listed on the following pages.

ARNICA *Arnica montana*

Also known as leopard's bane, this vivid yellow alpine flower has many well-documented medicinal uses. The arnica flower looks like a spindly yellow daisy, but it is the plant's roots that are of most use to us. From the root we can extract tincture of arnica, a powerful compound containing the bitter yellow substance called arnicin. Unlike its flowers, the root also contains tannins as well as several minerals. Tincture of arnica is available from most chemists and is extremely useful for applying to bruises (every first-aid kit should contain a bottle). It works by stimulating the circulation, and arnica cream is one of the most effective remedies for preventing a bruise from turning blue. I use a homoeopathic arnica cream almost daily on my children's bumps and bruises. Tincture of arnica is toxic, so it is for external use only and must not be swallowed. However, an extremely diluted form of arnica as tablets is available from homoeopathic suppliers and this is an excellent remedy for shock, or any emotional or physical injury. A safe, highly effective treatment, arnica tablets are especially recommended for children's tumbles, childbirth and minor accidents. See page 140 for details of homoeopathic suppliers and practitioners.

CHAMOMILE (German) *Matricaria chamomilla*

This herb takes its name from the Greek *kamai* (ground) and *melon* (apple) because of the sweet apple-like fragrance it releases when trodden on. Traditionally used to make scented lawns, chamomile is a low-growing, ground-covering herb with many practical uses. There are many varieties, but aromatherapists prefer *Matricaria chamomilla*, or German chamomile, which produces a highly prized blue oil.

The secret to this plant's success are substances called azulenes which have skin-soothing and anti-inflammatory properties. Natural azulenes are also believed to relieve pain, improve skin tissues and stimulate the immune-boosting activity of white blood cells. Azulenes can also found in the herb yarrow (see page 48).

Natural German chamomile also contains another extract called alpha-bisabolol, which is used in many skincare preparations for its uniquely soothing action on the skin. Studies at the University of Bonn in Germany have shown alpha-bisabolol to have both painkilling and anti-inflammatory properties. Trials have illustrated that it helps repair sun-damaged and chemically injured skin tissues, and that there is a proven basis for using chamomile extract to help wound healing.

The medicinal properties of natural chamomile are concentrated in the yellow centre of its flowers, and this is the part that is dried and turned into a sedative herb tea. Other parts of the plant, such as the whole flower heads and the leaves, are useful as a tonic and can be added to a bath to relieve tired, aching muscles.

Chamomile flowers are also useful as a gentle hair dye and bring a glossy sheen to naturally blonde hair. Chamomile tea-bags are a useful and convenient way of making herbal infusions and also make a soothing drink that helps the digestion. Medical herbalists often use chamomile internally to treat tension headaches, insomnia and nervous digestive disorders. The herb is also used frequently in children's remedies as it can help to calm and relieve many infant conditions including colic, teething and hyperactivity. Pure chamomile concentrate is available in liquid form from healthfood shops for adding to skincare recipes or using in healing compresses.

VIOLET *Viola odorata*

The violet is well known for its sweet, heady fragrance, which sadly fades as soon as the flowers are picked. This is due to its chemical composition which contains the volatile substance ionine, from which the name violet is derived. Violet herbal extracts have anti-inflammatory properties and are useful as a skin soother. A diluted version can also be used as a mouthwash for throat and mouth infections. Medical herbalists may use extracts from the flowers and leaves internally, as a powerful expectorant to treat respiratory and lung disorders.

WITCH HAZEL *Hamamelis virginiana*

Historically used to prevent internal bleeding, witch hazel extract is a useful astringent that also soothes the skin. It is one of the most widely used plants in Western medicine and the leaves contain high levels of a tannin, hamamelitannin, which gives them astringent properties and a healing action on veins. Tannins occur widely in nature and are used to heal the skin. They are responsible for binding protein in the skin to form a tight layer which is resistant to disease. This separates the bacteria which have settled on the skin and protects against potential irritation.

Witch hazel lotion is made from the leaves and twigs of the plant and is available from most chemists. Although this contains only ten per cent tannins and up to fifteen per cent alcohol, it is a handy ingredient for homemade skin fresheners, especially for inflamed skin conditions, compresses to heal wounds and soothing face masks.

Witch hazel capsules are also prescribed for internal use by medical herbalists to treat problems with veins and capillaries, including varicose veins, piles and broken thread veins on the face. Compresses made from witch hazel are also an effective external remedy for haemorrhoids (piles) and other cases of swelling.

YARROW *Achillea millefolium*

A tall herb with attractive feathery foliage and white flowers, yarrow gets its name from the Latin for 'thousand-leaf'. It is traditionally held that Aphrodite persuaded Achilles to dress his wounds with yarrow at the siege of Troy and it has since been associated with love and loyalty, especially for those injured in battle. Yarrow has been used by generations of wounded soldiers up until the Great War. It is well-known as a healing herb and even helps other plants nearby resist attacks from disease and pests.

Yarrow has astringent properties and is useful for pepping up a poor circulation and for improving skin tone. It also contains azulenes, the skin soothers found in some other herbs, notably chamomile. Culpeper used yarrow to prevent hair loss and modern herbalists regard yarrow as a useful all-round tonic that can also help to lower blood pressure. Externally, an infusion of yarrow leaves and flowers can be used as an effective skin tonic, and is useful for soothing sore skin conditions. It is also efficient at promoting wound healing and improving the skin's own micro-circulation.

ESSENTIAL OILS

In addition to plant extracts made from flowers, leaves and roots, many botanicals also contain essential oils which are remarkably effective in beauty recipes. Essential oils can be defined in two ways: their scientific explanation is that many plants contain high concentrations of volatile oils which give plants their distinctive flavours and aromas. These aromatic, essential or volatile oils are made up from a wide variety of different chemical constituents. A single essential oil may contain as many as fifty individual ingredients, including substances such as phenol, carvacrol, linalol and geraniol.

Aromatherapists, who use essential oils for therapeutic massage, are more likely to adopt a less clinical approach when it comes to defining essential oils. They often describe them as the 'life force' or 'soul' of the plant and believe that each essential oil has different characteristics and uses. Whether you take the more pragmatic and analytical approach, or prefer to follow the folklore, there is no doubt that essential oils can be extremely useful in caring for the body and encouraging well-being.

Essential oils can be extracted from plants in two main ways – by using either steam or solvent distillation. Steam distillation involves placing the plant material in a flask, heating to a high temperature and collecting the steam. As the steam cools and turns back into water, the essential oil from the plant floats to the surface where it can be collected. Steam distillation is the best method for extracting pure essential oils and most of the expensive varieties are extracted this way. The other method of solvent extraction is faster and involves placing the plant material in a flask and mixing with a chemical solvent such as hexane. The mixture is stirred and heated to release the essential oils from the plant before the solvent is evaporated away. Solvent extraction is common in the perfume industry, where natural flower fragrances are still used by some of the more expensive scents. However, it is not the best method for producing essential oils for skincare as traces of the solvent are invariably left behind in the oil.

Technically, anything that has been produced by solvent extraction should be called an 'absolute' and not an 'essential' oil. Common examples of these include rose absolute or jasmine absolute, which are extremely rare to find as essential oils made by steam distillation.

The main problem when buying essential oils is knowing exactly what is inside the bottle. Always look for the words 'pure essential oil', on the label which mean that the oil has not been diluted with a cheaper vegetable oil before bottling. Some oils are sold as 'aromatherapy oils' or 'fragrance oils' and should not be confused with genuine, highly concentrated essential oils.

Most healthfood shops stock reputable ranges and there is also a list of reliable mail-order suppliers at the back of the book. Another safety check is to make sure that your supplier is registered with EOTA (the Essential Oil Trade Association) as their members are regularly checked for quality control. If in doubt, go by the price. Essential oils are not cheap and in most cases you do get what you pay for.

However, because they are only used in tiny amounts, a good-quality essential oil will last a long time if kept cool and dark, and most oils have many health and beauty uses. All essential oils are naturally antiseptic and many are also naturally antibiotic. Some even

NATURAL SKIN SCIENCE

CLEANSERS AND SKIN TONICS

PROBLEM SOLVERS AND SKIN SAVERS

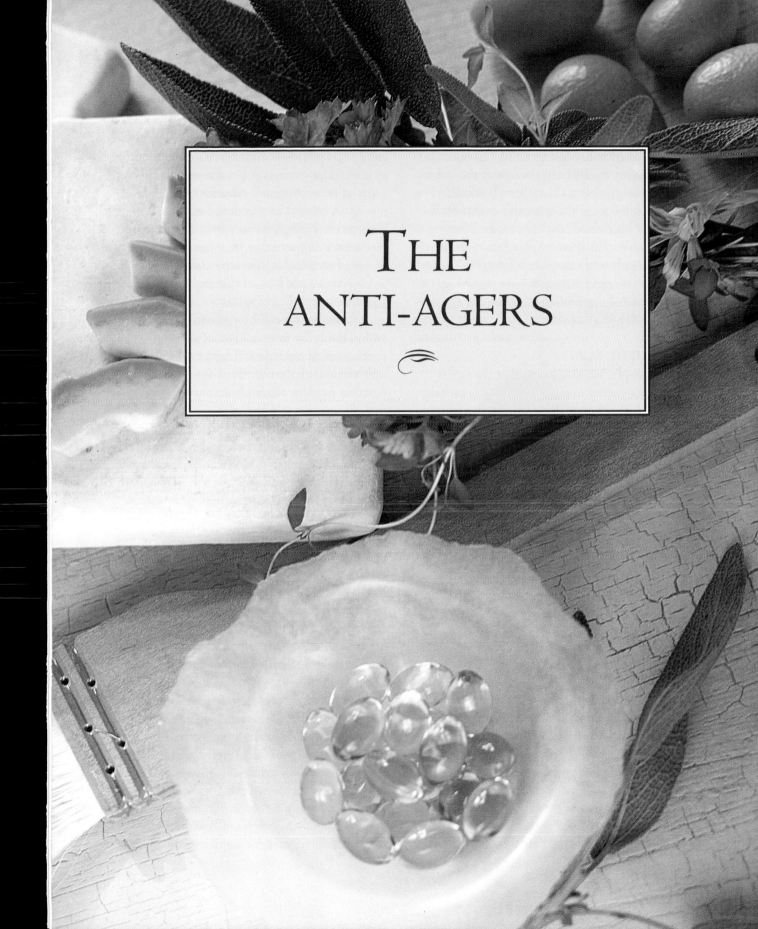

THE
ANTI-AGERS

BATHS AND BODY CARE

HAND AND FOOT CARE

At-Home Manicure

nail polish remover
cotton wool pads
nail scissors
emery board or nail file
Cuticle Cream (page 123)
rubber hoof stick
orange sticks
Orange Blossom Massage
   Cream (page 124)

Regular manicures are one of the easiest beauty salon treatments to carry out at home and will make all the difference to the long-term state of our hands and nails. Aim to give the hands a weekly manicure.

● Wash hands and nails in warm, soapy water and dry thoroughly.

● Remove any nail polish with remover on cotton wool pads.

● Trim long nails with nail scissors and file into a smooth oval shape, using an emery board or non-metal nail file. Avoid 'sawing' backwards and forwards as this weakens the nail. The best way to file the nails is in one direction only.

● After filing, rinse the fingertips in warm water and pat dry.

● Apply a small amount of Cuticle Cream around each nail and massage into the cuticle and base of the nail. Leave for a few minutes for the cream to penetrate and soften the skin.

● Next, take the rubber hoof stick and gently push back the cuticle from around each nail. Never force the skin back and avoid cutting or poking the cuticle as this can pierce the skin and lead to infections. When you have been around each cuticle, take an orange stick and wipe around the base of each nail to remove traces of cuticle cream.

● Apply a generous dollop of Orange Blossom Massage Cream and work into the fingers, palms and wrists. Each hand contains twenty-eight small bones and a complex network of muscles and tendons, so spend at least 10 minutes giving the hands a gentle massage. This not only releases tension and loosens up stiff joints but also increases blood circulation and keeps the skin feeling supple and smooth.

At-Home Pedicure

nail polish remover
cotton wool pads
footbath or washing-up
bowl
stiff nail brush
soap or Soapwort Cleanser
(page 77)
small towel
nail scissors
emery board or nail file
Cuticle Cream (page 123)
rubber hoof stick
cuticle clippers
Orange Blossom Massage
Cream (page 124)
talcum powder

Aim to give your feet a pedicure at least once a month to keep calluses, corns and bunions at bay.

● Begin by removing any nail polish from the toenails with remover and cotton wool pads.
● Half-fill the footbath or washing-up bowl with warm water and soak the feet for at least 5 minutes to allow the skin to warm and soften.
● Gently scrub the feet and toes with a stiff nail brush and soap or Simple Soapwort Cleanser.
● Dry the feet and toes thoroughly and trim long nails by cutting straight across with a small pair of nail scissors.
● Smooth any rough edges of the nails with an emery board or non-metal nail file.
● Apply a small amount of Cuticle Cream to each toenail and massage into the cuticles.
● Use a rubber hoof stick to gently encourage the cuticles

away from the nail bed, but be careful not to jab or poke too vigorously as this can pierce the skin and lead to infections. Use a sharp pair of cuticle clippers to cut away any small pieces of dead cuticle, but take care not to snip any living tissue.
● Spend the next 10 minutes massaging the feet with a generous helping of Orange Blossom Massage Cream – you will be rewarded for your efforts afterwards when your feet feel as though they are walking on air.
● Finally, dust in between the toes with talcum powder (you can make your own by mixing together equal quantities of arrowroot and cornflour, scented with small pieces of chopped orange and lemon peel).

In between treatments you can encourage healthy feet, ankles and toes by following these six steps to healthier feet.
● Switch heel heights during the day to give the feet and calves a break. If you wear high heels during the day, slip into a pair of pumps in the evening.
● Invest in a corrugated foot roller to give the feet a reflexology-style work-out during the day. Simply move the feet along

the roller to stimulate the nerve endings on the soles of the feet.
● Use a rich moisture cream on your feet at night and wake up to softer toes.
● Always wear well-fitting shoes and have your feet professionally measured from time to time when choosing a new pair, in case of change.
● Apply a daily dab of Cuticle Cream or almond oil to the toenails to keep cuticles soft

and well conditioned.
● Always trim toenails straight across, never down at the sides, to prevent in-growing toenails.

HERBAL
HAIR CARE

BY THE SAME AUTHOR

Vital Oils *(Vermilion)*

Save Your Skin with Vital Oils *(Vermilion)*

Eat Yourself Beautiful *(BBC Publications)*

Liz Earle's ACE Plan *(Boxtree)*

Weight Loss For Life *(Boxtree)*

Liz Earle's Bikini Diet *(Boxtree)*

Liz Earle's Lifestyle Guide *(Boxtree)*

Liz Earle's Quick Guides to *(Boxtree)*:

Acne

Antioxidants

Aromatherapy

Beating Cellulite

Beating PMS

Cod Liver Oil

Detox

Dry Skin & Eczema

Evening Primrose Oil

Food Allergies

Food Combining

Food Facts

Hair Loss

Healthy Menopause

Healthy Pregnancy

Herbs for Health

Juicing

Post Natal Health

Successful Slimming

Vitamins & Minerals

Youthful Skin

LIZ EARLE'S NATURAL SKINCARE

For further information about Liz Earle's own range of ethical skincare made without petro-chemicals but with high levels of naturally active ingredients, send a large stamped addressed envelope to Liz Earle, PO Box 7832, London SW15 6YA, United Kingdom. Or telephone Freephone 0800 413318.

Liz Earle skincare

No petro-chemicals

No chemical sunscreens

No animal testing

Every purchase supports charities